MW01681483

Holy Cow Cookbook

Kristen Barrett

Copyright Page

Holy Cow Cookbook

ISBN: 979-8-234-04990-2

Published by:
Kristen Barrett Publishing

This cookbook was compiled and edited by Kristen Barrett from recipes shared by members and friends of Seattle Christian Church. Unless otherwise noted, Scripture quotations are taken from the Holy Bible. All rights to specific translations are reserved by their respective publishers.

Printed in the United States of America.

Contents

Acknowledgements

As curator of *Holy Cow Cookbook*, I'd like to give a special thanks to the members of Seattle Christian Church and the many recipe contributors who generously shared their family favorites. This cookbook is a celebration of community, tradition, and the joy of sharing meals together. Thank you to those whose culinary creativity fill these pages with love and flavor:

Allison (Michi) Arakawa
Greg Barrett
Mona Borgens
Heidi Blake
Jennifer Blake Rivera
Derron Calvin
Lyn-Felice Calvin
JD DeLeon
Juanita Diaz
Mitch Edwards
Patience Edwards
MeLinda Harvey
Edwina Kamara
Donna Kennedy
Fred Ollie
Lennaea Sood
Marisa Stone
Edwin Tablit
Kylie Thornton
Nina ThyNguyen
Deanna Timmen
Josh Timmen
Lisa Wright
...and to all of the many others that prefer to remain anonymous donors, thank you!

Introduction

From Our Table to Yours:

Acts 2:46–47 reminds us that the early church *"broke bread in their homes and ate together with glad and sincere hearts."* "From the very beginning, gathering around the table has been part of what binds believers together. This cookbook is a celebration of that spirit.

Within these pages you will find recipes lovingly shared by the people of Seattle Christian Church – dishes prepared for potlucks, holidays, new babies, grieving families, celebrations, and ordinary weeknight dinners. Each recipe carries more than ingredients. It carries stories, traditions, and the quiet faithfulness of those who serve their families and their church through hospitality.

Food has a beautiful way of drawing us close. Around kitchen counters and dining room tables, prayers are whispered, laughter is shared, burdens are lightened, and memories are made. It is our hope that these recipes will not only fill your table but also warm your home and strengthen your fellowship. This cookbook has been created as a fundraiser to support SCC and the ministries that reach far beyond our walls. By purchasing and sharing it, you are helping invest in the continued work of the church while also carrying a piece of our community into your own home.

Whether you are a longtime member, a friend of SCC, or someone discovering this collection from afar, we pray these recipes bless you richly…from our table to yours.

From Pastor Kristen's Kitchen

Coming from Italian roots, I was raised in a family where gathering around the table and sharing great food was one of the strongest expressions of love. Conversations would overlap as everyone talked at once, laughter filling the room. The warmth in the air—mixed with the aroma of authentic home-cooked meals—created memories that have stayed with me my whole life. Laughter, love, and full bellies are what I cherish most about our family gatherings growing up. From feasting on our fresh-caught crab at the family beach house, *Family Tides*, to making my husband's Grandma Flora's homemade ravioli for holiday celebrations, we have been creating memories and building a legacy that has carried on for generations.

I remember when my husband, Greg, first inherited Grandma Flora's ravioli recipe. We struggled to read her handwriting, and the portions were big enough to feed an entire village! Over the years, we've managed to tailor the recipe down to a normal portion size and even conquered the challenge of making our own ravioli noodles from scratch. I think we would make Grandma Flora proud. Greg is honored to share his 3-Meat Ravioli recipe in the Main Dish section. We can't promise your fingers won't end up sticky or that your kitchen won't be covered in flour by the end—but that's part of the fun.

One of the greatest blessings at Seattle Christian Church is the way potluck meals bring our church family together. It reminds me so much of how my own family has gathered over the years to break bread and fellowship with one another.

On the first Sunday of each month, we are blessed with the opportunity to sit down as a church family and enjoy lunch together after service. Each year we also gather for a Thanksgiving potluck, where I've had the joy of exploring the incredible flavors within our community. More than once, I've found myself trying to track down a recipe months later from something I tasted and loved, such as the Sweet Potato casserole, now found in our Side Dish section. Eventually, I realized it was time to gather these wonderful recipes together—so I wouldn't have to wait a whole year, or travel further than my own kitchen, to enjoy them again.

Although I can't share every recipe I grew up with, I wanted to create a collection where some of our favorites could be passed along—without getting carried away and filling every page!

One of my son Eli's favorites is my Gingersnap Cookies, which you'll find in the Dessert section. We make them together every Christmas season. What started as a treat that we shared with our extended family has now become one of the staple desserts we bring to church potlucks. These days, I often find myself making triple batches to feed all of the eager mouths waiting for them.

My other son, Aden, loves Mexican food. Even though my roots are Italian, I've worked hard to perfect a Pozole Rojo recipe that meets his full approval. Before I finally perfected it, my friends had nicknamed it "Fire Soup." They were my brave taste-testers as I experimented with different chiles, sometimes leaving their mouths burning from an over-seasoned batch. You'll find that new and improved Pozole Rojo recipe in the Soups & Stews section.

Whether these meals are cherished traditions passed down from generation to generation or recipes discovered more recently and lovingly adapted with someone's own creative touch, the generous hearts who contributed them have filled the pages of the *Holy Cow Cookbook* with unique and delicious ideas.

At Seattle Christian Church, we take great pride in our multi-ethnic church family, and these pages reflect the beautiful diversity of flavors and traditions within our community.

As you use this cookbook to create memories in your own home—or to bring a dish that becomes the hit of your next potluck—my prayer is that you will feel the love that went into every recipe shared by my family and the wonderful members of Seattle Christian Church. May it bring laughter, conversation, full hearts and full bellies around your table for years to come.

After all, some of life's most meaningful moments happen not just in the sanctuary, but around the table.

Appetizers & Small Plates

"She rises while it is yet night and gets food for her household..."
Proverbs 31:15

Warm Olive & Green Chile Dip

From the kitchen of Kristen Barrett

Ingredients:

1 can diced Black Olives
1 can diced Green Chiles
¾ cup Mayonnaise
¼ cup Sour Cream
1 cup grated Cheddar Cheese (recommend Sharp White Cheddar or a blend of Monterey jack & cheddar)
Splash of Lime Juice
Pinch of Smoked Paprika

Instructions:

Preheat oven to 350°F. Mix ingredients and place into small oven-safe dish. Bake for 20-25 minutes. Serve with tortilla chips, sliced baguette bread or crostini.

Rob's Artichoke Dip

From the kitchen of Heidi Blake

Ingredients:

2 16-oz cans Artichoke Hearts, drained (not marinated)
1 cup Sour Cream
1 cup Mayonnaise
1 8-oz package Cream Cheese
1 Tbsp Dillweed (ideally fresh)
2 cloves Garlic, minced
1 ½ cups freshly grated Parmesan
1 4-oz can mild Green Chiles (optional)
French Baguette, Pita Chips and/or Tortilla Chips for scooping

Instructions:

Preheat oven to 350°F. Combine sour cream, mayonnaise and cream cheese until well blended. Add dillweed, garlic and 1 cup of the parmesan, stir. Chop artichoke hearts. (For a creamier dip, puree 1 can of the artichoke hearts). Add to the cream mixture. Pour into oven-safe baking dish. Top with remaining ½ cup of parmesan cheese. Bake for 1 hour.
**This may bubble over in the oven so we suggest you put something underneath dish.
Serve with sliced baguette, pita chips or tortilla chips.

Sausage Stuffed Mushrooms

From the kitchen of Kristen Barrett

Ingredients:

1 large container White Mushrooms
¼ lb Breakfast Sausage (or 5-6 sausage patties), cooked
3-4 Tbsp Butter
¼ cup Italian Bread Crumbs
½ cup Parmesan Cheese
2 cloves Garlic, minced
3 stems Green Onion, finely chopped
2 Tbsp Olive oil
Salt & Pepper to taste

Instructions:

Preheat oven to 350°F. Wash mushrooms and trim off dirty ends of stems. Remove stems and pulse in food processor with garlic and cooked sausage. Sauté mixture on med-low heat with butter, bread crumbs and parmesan. Mix until blended. Gently fold in green onion. Remove from heat.
Meanwhile, toss mushroom caps in olive oil and salt & pepper. Arrange on cookie sheet, hollow side up, and fill each cap with small, equal amounts of filling mixture. Bake 15-20 minutes or until caps are tender. Transfer to dish and enjoy!

Clean Guilt-Free Layered Dip

From the kitchen of Mona Borgens

Ingredients:

Layer 1 - Base
1 can organic Refried Black or Pinto Beans, no added sugar
8 ounces green hatch chiles

Layer 2 - Greek Yogurt "Cream"
1½ cups plain full-fat Greek Yogurt
1 Tbsp Taco Seasoning made from: cumin, chili powder, garlic powder, onion powder, paprika, oregano, sea salt
½ Lime, juiced

Layer 3 - Avocado
3 ripe Avocados
1 Lime, juiced
1 clove Garlic, finely minced
Cilantro, chopped (optional)
Sea Salt and Pepper, to taste
Layer 4 - Salsa and fresh toppings
1-1½ cups clean ingredient Salsa (no sugar or canola/soy oil)
½-1 cup Romaine or Cabbage, finely shredded
½ cup diced Tomatoes or Pico de Gallo

Top with:
A sprinkle of crumbled Cotija or a small amount of organic Cheddar
Slices of jalapeño
¼ cup finely diced Red Onion or Green Onion
1 large can sliced Black Olives

Stack each of these layers in a shallow dish with rim. Serve with tortilla chips. Serves 8-10 people.

Baked Creamy Artichoke Spinach Dip

Anonymous

Ingredients:

1 8-oz package Cream Cheese, softened
½ cup Sour Cream
¼ cup Mayonnaise
1 cup shredded Mozzarella
½ cup grated Parmesan
1 cup chopped Spinach (fresh or thawed frozen, squeezed dry)
1 cup Artichoke Hearts, drained & chopped
2 cloves Garlic, minced
Salt & Pepper, to taste

Instructions:

Preheat oven to 375°F. Mix cream cheese, sour cream, and mayo until smooth.
Stir in shredded cheeses, spinach, artichokes, garlic, salt, and pepper. Spread into a small baking dish.
Bake 20–25 minutes until bubbly and lightly golden on top.
Serve with toasted baguette slices, crackers, or tortilla chips.

Grandma Lujan's Cracker Spread

From the kitchen of Donna Kennedy

Ingredients:

1 8-oz package Cream Cheese
½ cup Sour Cream
2 Tbsp Milk
2 tsp Onion, minced
¼ cup chopped Walnuts
2 ½ ounces Dried Beef

Instructions:

Preheat oven to 350°F. Blend all ingredients together in a 2-quart 8x8 Pyrex dish and bake in the oven for 30 minutes. Serve with crackers of your choice.

Nancie's Salmon Patties

From the kitchen of Donna Kennedy

Ingredients:

2 large (13-14 oz) cans Red Salmon
1 large can Pink Salmon
3-4 Eggs
¼ cup Mayonnaise
½ Tbsp Lemon Pepper
¼ cup Chopped Chives
Salt, to taste
1 ½ cups Saltine Crackers
Lemon wedges for serving

Instructions:

Drain the salmon in a colander and remove the skin and bones as much as possible. Then flake the Salmon so it's all uniform pieces. Set aside.
In a bowl, mix eggs, lemon pepper, Mayo, Chives and you could also add a little lemon and salt to taste.
In a large zip lock bag, crush about 1 ½ cups saltine crackers. Mix all together in a large bowl and form into patties. (adjust seasoning, eggs and crackers as needed).
Fry in hot oil till browned, flip and brown the other side and drain on paper towel.
Ready to serve with fresh lemon wedges.

Chorizo Stuffed Dates Wrapped in Bacon

From the kitchen of Mona Borgens

Ingredients:

6 slices Bacon, cut crosswise into thirds
1 link Chorizo Sausage, sliced
18 pitted Dates
18 Toothpicks, soaked in water for 20 minutes

Instructions:

Preheat oven to 375°F. Line sheet pan with parchment paper. Using a paring knife, make lengthwise slice down each date and fold it open like a book. Place chorizo into each date, fold closed and wrap each date with a piece of bacon. Secure each date with a toothpick.
Arrange dates onto baking sheet and bake for 15-20 minutes, until bacon is cooked thoroughly. Yields 18 pieces.

Bacon Wrapped Apricots with Sage

From the kitchen of Mona Borgens

Ingredients:

24 small fresh Sage Leaves
24 large Dried Apricots
8 slices Bacon, cut crosswise into thirds
2 Tbsp Pure Maple Syrup
Toothpicks, for serving

Instructions:

Preheat oven to 375°F. Place a sage leaf on each apricot, wrap with a piece of bacon, and place seam-side down onto baking sheet. Bake 6-8 minutes per side, until bacon begins to crisp. Remove from oven and brush with maple syrup. Serve with toothpicks.

Classic Tomato Bruschetta

From the kitchen of Mitch Edwards

Ingredients:

1 large French Baguette or Italian Loaf, sliced into ½ -in rounds
6-7 Roma Tomatoes, seeded and diced
2 cloves Garlic, minced
¼ cup fresh Basil, thinly sliced or "chiffonade"
2 Tbsp Extra Virgin Olive Oil
1 tsp Balsamic Glaze
Salt and Pepper, to taste
1 whole Garlic clove (peeled, for rubbing on the bread)

Instructions:

Prep the Tomatoes: In a bowl, toss the diced tomatoes, minced garlic, olive oil, and basil. Season with salt and pepper to taste. Let this sit for at least 10–15 minutes at room temperature. This allows the juices to develop; but make sure to drain any excess liquid before topping onto the bread so it doesn't get soggy.
Toast the Bread: Brush both sides of your bread slices lightly with olive oil. Grill them on a pan or bake at 400°F (200°C) for about 5 minutes until they are golden and crisp.
The Garlic Rub: This is the most important step! While the bread is still warm and scratchy, take the whole garlic clove and rub it across the surface of each slice. The toast acts like a grater and picks up a perfect, subtle garlic flavor.
Assemble the bruschetta by scooping the tomato mixture generously onto each slice of the toasted bread.
Finish with a drizzle of balsamic glaze or a sprinkle of Parmesan cheese over the top right before serving.

Tuna Melt Quesadilla

From the kitchen of Edwin Tablit

Ingredients:

1 can of Tuna, drained
3 heaping Tbsp Limon Mayo
1 Tbsp Paprika
1 Tbsp Garlic Powder
Sprinkle of Salt and Pepper
1 can Corn, drained
1 Tbsp Pickled Jalapeños, chopped
4 Corn Tortillas
2 cups shredded Tillamook Medium Cheese
Green Onion for garnish

Optional Greek Yogurt dipping sauce:
$^1/_3$ cup Greek Yogurt
1 tsp Paprika
1 tsp Garlic powder
1 tsp Cumin

Instructions:

In small bowl, add tuna, mayo, corn, chopped jalapeño, paprika, garlic powder, salt and pepper; mix.
Heat up 4 tortillas for 3 min on medium heat and flip. Put shredded cheese on top of each tortilla. Add 2 Tbsp of mixture on top of 2 of the cheesed tortillas. Place the 2 remaining cheesed tortillas on top (cheese side down.
(Save the rest of mixture for the next time you make this)
Garnish with green onion. Enjoy with Greek Yogurt dipping sauce. Makes 2 tuna melt quesadillas, and left over tuna.

Man Nuggets

From the kitchen of Josh Timmen

Ingredients:

4 boneless Chicken Breasts
1 cup Mayonnaise (or more, to taste)
1-2 cups Italian-Style Breadcrumbs (to taste)
1 tsp Garlic Salt

Instructions:

Preheat oven to 375°F (190°C). Lightly grease or line a baking sheet.
Rinse chicken and pat dry. Spread mayonnaise over one side of each chicken breast.
Mix breadcrumbs and garlic salt. Press the mayo-coated side of the chicken into the mixture until fully covered (you shouldn't see mayonnaise).
Place chicken on the baking sheet, coated side up. Bake 25–35 minutes, until golden brown and the internal temperature reaches 165°F.

Optional variation (stuffed):

For a stuffed version, cut each chicken breast in half lengthwise (or butterfly it) and add deli ham and Swiss cheese (about 2–4 slices each). Close the chicken around the filling, then continue with the mayonnaise-and-breadcrumb coating and bake as directed.

Side Dish

"I am the bread of life. Whoever comes to me will never go hungry."
John 6:35

Italian Pasta Salad

From the kitchen of Kristen Barrett

Ingredients:

1 package Bowtie Pasta or Spiral Pasta (I prefer tri-colored for flare), cooked and cooled
1 package thick-sliced, small Genoa Salami, diced
1 jar Marinated Artichoke Hearts, chopped
1 small can sliced Black Olives (you can also add some sliced Kalamata Olives)
8 ounces fresh Mozzarella, cubed
3-4 Green Onion stalks, diced
Small handful Basil leaves, diced
¼ cup Sun-dried tomatoes, diced
Creamy Italian dressing, add enough until smooth consistency and flavor achieved.

Instructions:

Mix all ingredients in large bowl, cover and keep refrigerated until serving. Best if prepared 2-4 hours before serving. You may need to add more dressing before serving if pasta appears dried out once it's had time to soak up the dressing.
Goes great with summer barbecue's and potlucks.

Arugula Salad with Chicken

From the kitchen of Lyn-Felice Calvin

Ingredients:

Dressing:
2 Tbsp Olive Oil
2 Tbsp fresh Lemon Juice
1 tsp Honey
½ tsp Kosher Salt
½ tsp freshly ground Black Pepper

4 cups Arugula
¼ cup shaved Parmesan Cheese

Additional Optional Toppings, to taste:
Red Onion, thinly sliced
Kalamata Olives, pitted and sliced
Artichoke Hearts (Marinated), drained & chopped
Cucumber, sliced
Grilled Chicken Breasts, sliced

Instructions:

Mix together the ingredients for the dressing and shake together in a jar. Refrigerate until ready for use.
Place arugula, olives, cucumber, artichoke hearts and onions in a bowl and toss together with some of the dressing. Top with chicken and parmesan cheese. Add more dressing, to taste. Extra dressing can be stored in the refrigerator for future use.

Baby Pea Salad with Water Chestnuts

From the kitchen of Heidi Blake

Ingredients:

2 16-oz package Frozen Baby Peas, thawed
1 lb Bacon, sliced and sauteed (Peppered Bacon is wonderful)
4 stalks Celery, chopped
½ cup Green Onion, sliced
1 5-oz can Water Chestnuts, drained & chopped
½ cup Sour Cream
1 small package Uncle Dan's Ranch Dressing mix
$^1/_3$ cup Light House Blue Cheese Salad Dressing (Optional)
Dash of Salt & Pepper

Instructions:

Mix sour cream with Uncle Dan's mix. Let sit overnight for best flavor.
In large bowl, combine thawed peas, celery, onion, $^2/_3$ of the bacon and water chestnuts. Pour both dressings over the mixture and stir gently, as not to smash the peas. Chill, then top with extra bacon.

**Note: This recipe can be modified by adding Olives, Tomatoes, Red Onion, Cucumber or Hard Boiled Eggs.

Pancit Bihon (Rice Noodles)

Anonymous

Ingredients:

8 ounces Rice noodles (Pancit Bihon)
1 lb Chicken Breast or Pork, thinly sliced
3 Tbsp Soy Sauce
1 Tbsp Oyster Sauce
1 Tbsp Fish Sauce (optional)
3 Tbsp Cooking Oil
4 Cloves Garlic, minced
1 medium Onion, sliced
2 medium Carrots, julienned
½ head Cabbage, shredded
½ cup Green Beans, trimmed & sliced
2 cups Chicken Broth
1 tsp Ground Black Pepper
Lemon wedges, for serving
Chopped green onions, for garnish

Instructions:

Soak the noodles in water for 10-15 minutes until softened. Drain and set aside.
In a large skillet or wok, heat cooking oil over medium heat. Add sliced chicken or pork and cook until browned. Then, add the garlic & onion. Cook until fragrant & translucent.
Add carrots, green beans and cabbage. Stir fry for 3-5 minutes.
Add soy sauce, oyster sauce, fish sauce (if using) and chicken broth. Stir well to combine.

When it starts boiling, Add the soaked noodles & stir until it well combined with the sauce and vegetables. Cook for 5 to 7 minutes. Stirring occasionally until the noodles are fully cooked and have absorbed the liquid.

Season with ground black pepper. Taste!!

Add salt if you need it…

Japanese Namasu

From the kitchen of Michi Arakawa

Ingredients:

3 cups Cucumber, thinly sliced
½ tsp Salt
1 tsp Ginger, very finely chopped or ¼ tsp Ground Ginger
4 Tbsp Rice Vinegar
2 Tbsp Sugar

Instructions:

Partly peel cucumber lengthwise, leaving some green and slice very thinly creating circular thin slices. Salt cucumber slices and mix. Let stand 15 min. Combine remaining ingredients in another bowl to make sauce. Press cucumber to discard excess liquid from them; and add cucumber to sauce. Mix well. Chill and serve. Serves 6 people.

**Goes great with Chicken Katsu in Main Dish section.

Baked Beans

From the kitchen of Derron Calvin

Ingredients:

1 Onion, finely chopped
1 Green Bell Pepper, finely chopped
2-3 Celery Stalks, finely chopped
1 Jalapeño, finely chopped
1 lb Ground Hamburger (or Ground Turkey)
2 slices Bacon, chopped
2 large cans Bush's Baked Beans
1 Tbsp Ketchup
1 Tbsp Mustard
1 Tbsp Bar-B-Que Sauce
1 tsp Garlic Powder
1 tsp Onion Powder
Salt and Pepper, to taste

Instructions:

Sauté onion, bell pepper, celery and jalapeño until tender.
Add and cook ground meat and bacon. Strain out excess grease.
Add Bush's baked beans and heat through.
Add sauces and seasonings; mix and simmer on low for a while to allow flavors to come together!

Heidi's Special Carrots

From the kitchen of Heidi Blake

Ingredients:

2 cups lightly salted Water
2-3 lbs fresh Carrots, peeled and sliced in desired slice style
½ cup Parsley, chopped
½ cup Onion, finely chopped
½ stick of Butter
½ tsp fresh Ground Pepper
½ tsp of Knorr Aromat Seasoning
½ tsp Uncle Dan's Original Ranch Seasoning

Instructions:

Steam or boil carrots in salt water until slightly tender.
Meanwhile, in another large pot, melt butter.
Add chopped onions and sauté until translucent. Add parsley. Sauté another 2-3 minutes. Drain carrots and add to onions & parsley. Add seasonings and pepper. Mix and transfer to serving dish. Decorate with fresh sprig of parsley.
Serves 4-6 people.

Macaroni and Cheese

From the kitchen of Lisa Wright

Ingredients:

2 lbs of large Elbow Macaroni noodles
8 ounces Velveeta cheese
2-lb block of Tillamook extra sharp white cheddar, shredded
(Do not use pre-shredded cheese)
2-lb block of Tillamook cheddar cheese, shredded
8 cups of Extra Heavy Whipping
1 pint Half-and-Half Cream
1 stick of Butter
4 Tbsp of Flour
2 tsp each Johnny's Seasoning Salt & Black Pepper
2 tsp each Onion Powder & Garlic Powder
2 tsp Paprika
2 tsp Ground Mustard

Instructions:

Preheat oven to 400°F. Boil pasta in salted water until tender; drain and let cool in a large party size foil pan. In a large stockpot, melt stick of butter, add flour and all spices; cook for 4 minutes on medium heat. Slowly add the heavy cream and half & half. Heat on medium for 10 minutes.

Slowly whisk in all of the white cheddar and all but 2 cups of cheddar cheese.

Mix until all is well blended. Pour this cheese sauce into the pan of noodles, stirring it all together. Top it with the remaining 2 cups cheddar cheese and bake uncovered for 25 minutes.

Serves 6-10 people.

Fried Cabbage

From the kitchen of Sherry Hunter

Ingredients:

1 medium head of Cabbage
½ Yellow Onion
½ Bell Pepper (Green for bitter flavor or Red for sweetness)
3 Tbsp Oil
¼ cup Vegetable Broth
Garlic Salt or Seasoning Salt and Pepper, to taste

Instructions:

Chop onions, cabbage and bell pepper; sauté in oil on medium-high heat until tender. Add vegetable broth to prevent sticking and simmer until cabbage is soft (depending on how crisp you desire it). Add garlic salt and pepper.

**Note: You can also season it with the same seasonings that you use for preparing your meat main dish. Also goes great paired with rice and cornbread.

Michelle B's Best Sweet Potatoes

From the kitchen of Donna Kennedy

Ingredients:

2 29-oz cans Sweet Potatoes, well drained.
2 Eggs
½ cup Milk
1 ½ cup Brown Sugar (divided ¾ cups each)
1 tsp Vanilla
1 tsp Salt
½ tsp Cinnamon
¼ cup melted Butter + a bit more
½ cup Flour
1 cup Chopped Pecans

Instructions:

Preheat oven to 375°F. Grease 9x13 inch baking dish.
In a large bowl, mash sweet potatoes, mix in milk, eggs, ¾ cup brown sugar, vanilla, salt and cinnamon. Spread mixture in the baking dish.
In a separate bowl, making topping by mixing melted butter, flour, ¾ cup brown sugar, and then add the pecans.
Sprinkle this mixture over the top of the potato mixture in the baking dish.
Bake for 30-35 minutes.

Main Dish

"The eyes of all look to You, and You give them their food at the proper time. You open your hand and satisfy the desire of every living thing."
Psalm 145:15-16

Papa Bill's Chicken Marinade

From the kitchen of Kristen Barrett

Ingredients:

1 ½ cups Vegetable Oil
¾ cup Soy Sauce
¼ cup Worcestershire Sauce
½ cup Red Wine Vinegar
⅓ cup Lemon Juice
2 cloves Garlic, minced
2 Tbsp Dry Mustard
2 ½ tsp Salt
1 Tbsp Pepper
1 ½ tsp Parsley flakes
16-18 Bone-in Chicken Legs and/or Thighs

Instructions:

Mix all ingredients, pour over chicken and marinade in large Tupperware for 2 days in refrigerator, mixing periodically. Remove from marinade; cook chicken on a barbecue or smoker at 350°F. Watch carefully for flames, as vinegar makes it more flammable. Cook until internal temperature of chicken reads 165°F.
Serves 8-10 people.

Grandma's Cajun Meatloaf

From the kitchen of Marisa Stone

Ingredients:

1 tsp Salt
1 ½ tsp Cracked Black Pepper
½ tsp Cayenne Pepper
½ tsp Cumin
½ tsp Nutmeg
1 Bay Leaf
2 Tbsp Butter
¾ cup Onion, diced small
½ Green Bell Pepper, diced small
2 Garlic cloves, minced
1 large Carrot, diced small
½ Tbsp Tabasco Sauce
1 Tbsp Worcestershire Sauce
½ cup Milk
½ cup Catsup
1 ½ pounds Ground Beef
1 Egg beaten to blend

Instructions:

Preheat oven to 375°F. Combine first 6 ingredients in a small bowl, set aside. In sauce pan, Sauté onions in butter until softened. Add peppers, garlic and carrots until onions are translucent and peppers softened. Stir in spice mix, Tabasco and Worcestershire. Cook until thickened. Remove bay leaf. Mix in milk and catsup; heat through. Combine beaten egg, beef and onion mixture thoroughly. Shape into loaf on pan. Bake for 30 minutes, covered with foil, and then 30 minutes, uncovered.

Lasagna

From the kitchen of Lyn-Felice Calvin

Ingredients:

Sauce:
1 lb Ground Beef or Turkey
1 clove Garlic, crushed
1 tsp Sugar
1 Tbsp Basil, chopped
1 medium Onion, chopped
2 Tbsp Parsley, chopped
16-oz can Whole Tomatoes, not drained
16-oz can Tomato Sauce
2 whole Carrots (to soak in sauce to reduce acidity, then remove before constructing lasagna)

Ricotta Layer:
16-oz tub Ricotta Cheese
¼ cup Parmesan
1 Tbsp Parsley
1 Tbsp fresh Oregano (or 1 ½ tsp dried Oregano)

12 Lasagna Noodles
2 cups Mozzarella Cheese
¼ cup Parmesan Cheese

Instructions:

In large sauce pan, brown meat, onion and garlic; strain excess grease. Add all other sauce ingredients to meat mixture. Break down tomatoes. Bring to a boil, then simmer on low 1 hour until thickened. Remove whole carrots.

While sauce is simmering, in separate bowl, mix ingredients for the ricotta layer, refrigerate until ready to assemble lasagna.
Preheat oven to 350°F. Meanwhile, boil lasagna noodles as directed on packaging.
In 9x13 casserole dish, apply an even layer of meat sauce, noodles, ricotta cheese, sprinkle of mozzarella and parmesan.
Repeat layers until all noodles have been used and topped with sauce and sprinkles of mozzarella and parmesan (no ricotta on top layer of noodles).
Cover with foil and bake for 30 minutes. Uncover and bake another 15 minutes. Allow it to set-up for 5 minutes before slicing and serving.

Creamy Chicken

From the kitchen of Fred Ollie

Ingredients:

2 lbs boneless, skinless Chicken
1 10.5-oz can Cream of Chicken Soup
1 packet Good Seasons Italian Dressing dry mix
1 ½ cup Shredded Swiss Cheese
10.5 ounces Milk

Instructions:

Preheat oven to 350°F.
Place chicken in 9x13 inch pan. Sprinkle half of the Italian seasoning packet directly onto chicken. Flip chicken over and sprinkle the other half of the Italian seasoning packet on the chicken.
In a separate bowl, mix one can of cream of chicken soup and use that can to measure 10.5 ounces of milk; mix with soup.
Add in the Swiss cheese and stir together.
Pour the soup/cheese mixture over the chicken so that it covers the chicken entirely. Place the uncovered pan of chicken into the oven; bake for 30 to 45 minutes. Cooking time varies depending on the size of your chicken pieces.
Serve over rice and enjoy.

Fish & Chips

From the kitchen of Kristen Barrett

Ingredients:

1 filet Cod (or Halibut), sliced in 3-inch strips
1 cup Flour
6 Eggs
¼ cup Milk
1 cup Panko Breading
½ cup Fish-fry Breading mix (like Zatarains or Louisiana)
Generous amounts Lemon Pepper, Old Bay, Salt, to taste (or any other flavor combinations you may want)
Canola Oil (enough to fully submerge fish in deep fryer or pan)

For serving: Lemon wedges and Creamy Dill Pickle Sauce, for dipping (recipe included on next page)

Instructions:

Pour canola oil into deep fryer and warm to 350-375°F. Rinse and pat fish dry before slicing into desired chunks. In 3 shallow bowls, place flour and half of the seasonings in bowl #1; place eggs and milk in bowl #2, slightly beaten; and then mix panko, fish-fry breading and remaining seasonings in bowl #3.
Take each piece of fish and coat it in the flour mixture, then egg mixture, and then the breadcrumb mixture. Transfer to fryer and cook until breading turns a golden brown color and fish becomes flaky. Remove from oil; Strain off excess oil and place on paper towel lined pan.
**Pair with your favorite French fries and Deanna's Creamy Dill Pickle Tartar Sauce on the next page.

Creamy Dill Pickle Sauce (Tartar-Style)

From the kitchen of Deanna Timmen

Ingredients:

1 cup of real Mayonnaise
1 cup Dill Pickles, finely chopped
1 Tbsp fresh or frozen Dill or 1 Tbsp fresh Parsley, finely chopped
1 tsp Lemon Juice
1 tsp Sugar
¼ tsp freshly Ground Black Pepper
2 Tbsp Onion (optional), finely chopped

Instructions:

In a medium bowl, add the mayonnaise. Stir in the chopped dill pickles until evenly combined. Add the dill (or parsley), lemon juice, sugar, and black pepper.
If desired, mix in finely chopped onion. Stir well until smooth.
Cover and refrigerate for at least 30 minutes to let the flavors develop.
Store covered in the refrigerator for up to 5–7 days.

Coconut Thai Salmon

From the kitchen of Mona Borgens

Ingredients:

Salmon:
1 ½ lbs Salmon
1 Tbsp Brown Sugar
1 tsp Curry Powder
½ tsp Onion Powder
½ tsp Garlic Powder
½ tsp Kosher Salt (more for a larger filet)
1-2 tsp Olive Oil

Coconut Curry Sauce:
1 Tbsp Olive Oil
2 cloves Garlic, minced
1 small knob of Ginger, minced
1 Tbsp of Lemongrass Paste
1 Tbsp Brown Sugar
1 Tbsp Red Curry Paste
1 can Coconut Milk
2 Tbsp Fish Sauce or Soy Sauce
Lots of Lime Juice and Zest
3 cups fresh Spinach, chopped

For serving:
Cilantro, Basil, Mint, or other fresh herbs and rice

Instructions:

Preheat the oven to 475°F. Line a baking sheet with foil. Place one of the oven racks closer towards the top (about 6 inches).

Mix the spices and the olive oil to make a paste. Place the salmon, skin side down, onto baking sheet. Rub the paste liberally over the top portion of the salmon. Bake for 6-12 minutes (depends on salmon thickness and desired doneness - I usually opt for 8-10 minutes).

To make Coconut Curry Sauce: Heat the olive oil over medium heat. Add garlic, ginger and lemongrass; sauté for 5 minutes. Add brown sugar and curry paste; sauté for 3 minutes. Add coconut milk. Season with fish sauce, lime juice, and lime zest to taste. Add spinach; stir into the sauce until wilted. Place salmon over rice. Cover with sauce, lime juice, and fresh herbs.

Serves 3 to 5 people.

Spicy Penang Curry Bowl

From the kitchen of Mona Borgens

Ingredients:

For Curry Sauce:
1 Tbsp Coconut Oil
3 Tbsp Penang Curry Paste (store-bought or homemade)
1 Tbsp Natural Creamy Peanut Butter
1 ½ cups canned full-fat Coconut Milk (roughly 13.5 oz)
1 Tbsp Fish Sauce (or Soy Sauce for vegan version)
1 Tbsp Palm Sugar or Coconut Sugar
6 kaffir Lime Leaves (whole or torn; or ½ tsp Lime Zest)
2 tsp freshly squeezed Lime Juice
Cinnamon, to taste

Bowl Base:
1 small Red Bell Pepper, julienned
1 small Orange Bell Pepper, julienned
½ small Sweet Onion, thinly sliced
1 small Zucchini, sliced into half moons
1 cup Mushrooms, sliced
1 cup Broccoli Florets (or Snap Peas & Carrots)
8 ounces cooked Chicken Breast, Shrimp, or Tofu

Optional garnishes: fresh Thai basil, cilantro, sliced red chili (for added spice), lime wedges

Instructions:

Heat coconut oil in a deep skillet over medium heat. Add the curry paste and peanut butter; sauté for 2 minutes until fragrant and the paste begins to separate.

Add about half the can of coconut milk, stirring constantly until the sauce slightly thickens (3–5 minutes). Then add the rest of the milk, kaffir lime leaves, fish sauce, sugar and cinnamon. Simmer for 5 minutes.

Cook vegetables and protein: Add bell peppers, onions, mushrooms, zucchini, and broccoli or snap peas and carrots. Simmer until tender but still crisp, about 5–7 minutes. Add protein (chicken, shrimp, or tofu) and simmer until heated through. Stir in lime juice and taste for balance. Adjust sweetness, saltiness, or spice level as desired with additional sugar, fish sauce, or curry paste.

Assemble bowls: Spoon black rice or jasmine rice into serving bowls, ladle curry over the top, and garnish with fresh basil or cilantro.

Optional Add-Ins:

Add snap peas and carrots for more color and crunch.

Sticky brown rice - cauliflower rice.

Use a mix of brown and black rice for a hearty base.

Add a spoonful of chili oil or sriracha for an extra kick.

Poc Chuc

From the kitchen of Deanna Timmen

Ingredients:

Marinade:
3 lbs Pork Loin
1 head of Garlic, minced
1 cup Olive Oil
1 tsp of Salt
½ tsp Black Pepper
½ tsp Ground Cumin
½ cup sour Orange Juice (e.g. La Lechonera Naranja Agria)

Pico de Gallo:
4 Plum Tomatoes, diced
½ cup sour Orange Juice (e.g. La Lechonera Naranja Agria)
Salt to taste
1 tsp Dried Oregano (Mexican, if possible)
2 Red Onions, diced
1–2 Jalapeño(s), minced
1 cup Cilantro, chopped (add at time of serving)

Instructions:

Make Pico de Gallo: Mix diced onion and minced jalapeño with salt, oregano, and sour orange juice. Let sit while you dice tomatoes. Stir in tomatoes. Add cilantro right before serving. Marinate pork: (Optional) mix Brine 2 days ahead. Marinate pork at least overnight (or early the day of). Remove pork from marinade. Grill 2–4 minutes per side to medium-well, so that internal temperature reads 155–160°F. Slice thinly. Serve on corn tortillas with Pico, salsa, black beans, and avocado, or over rice.

Beef Tamale Pie

From the kitchen of Lisa Wright

Ingredients:

2 boxes of Jiffy Cornbread Mix
2 Eggs
2 Taco Bell Seasoning packets
2 lbs Ground Beef
½ cup Sour Cream
½ cup Whole Milk
1 7-oz can diced Green Chiles
1 10-oz can Enchilada Sauce
1 14-oz can Creamed Corn
3 cups shredded Colby Jack Cheese
1 4-oz can sliced Black Olives
½ cup Green Onions, diced
½ cup Tomatoes, diced
Sour cream on the side

Preheat oven to 375°F. In a frying pan, Brown ground beef; drain the grease and add packets of Taco Bell seasoning. Follow the directions on the packet.
In a mixing bowl, combine Jiffy cornbread mix and eggs, milk, creamed corn, sour cream and green chiles. Mix together.
Bake cornbread mixture in a buttered 9x13 inch baking dish for 20 minutes. Test with a toothpick to make sure it's cooked!
Use a wooden spoon and poke holes throughout the top of the cooked cornbread. Spread enchilada sauce on top. Add your cooked meat on top. Top with cheese, green onions and black olives. And bake for another 20 minutes.
When removed from oven, top with chopped tomatoes, onions and olives. And serve with sour cream.

Chicken Tamale Casserole

From the kitchen of Deanna Timmen

Ingredients:

1 14-oz King Arthur Gluten-Free Cornbread Mix
1 8.25-oz can Creamed Corn
1 Egg, lightly beaten
$^2/_3$ cup of Milk
6 Tbsp Butter, melted
2 cups shredded Mexican/Taco Cheese, divided
½ tsp Cumin
2–3 cups shredded cooked Chicken (Rotisserie)
10 ounces Red Enchilada Sauce (El Paso)
¼ cup of Sour Cream
1 4-oz can Green Chiles
1/8 tsp Cayenne Pepper
2 Green Onions, sliced

Toppings: Sour Cream, diced Tomato, Black Olives, Avocado, Cilantro

Instructions:

Preheat oven to 400°F. Grease a 9×13 inch pan. Mix cornbread mix, creamed corn, egg, milk, butter, 1 cup cheese, and cumin. Spread in pan; bake 20–25 minutes until set. Poke about 25 holes in baked cornbread, using a wooden-spoon handle.
Mix chicken, enchilada sauce, sour cream, green chiles, and cayenne. Spread chicken mixture over cornbread. Top with green onions and remaining cheese; bake 5–10 minutes. Slice and serve with desired toppings.
Serves 8 people.

Vegan Enchilada Casserole

From the kitchen of Lyn-Felice Calvin

Ingredients:

1 ½ cups Quinoa, cooked
1 ½ cups Brown Rice, cooked
1 can Black Beans, drained
2 Tbsp Jalapeño, finely diced
2 Green Onions, chopped (save some for the topping)
1 pound of Beyond Meat (optional)
1 packet McCormick Chipotle Taco Seasoning mix
1 Packet McCormick Enchilada Sauce mix
8-oz can Tomato Sauce
1 Roma Tomato, diced
⅓ cup fresh Cilantro, chopped
Salt and Pepper, to taste
Diced Avocado to serve on the side
8-oz can Sliced Olives

Note: If you can't find the Chipotle Taco Mix, use regular taco mix packet and use the juice from a can of chipotle chilies.

Instructions:

Preheat oven to 350°F. Cook the brown rice and quinoa ahead of time and use portions of each.
Brown the Beyond Meat in a skillet and add the Chipotle seasoning mix according to the packet directions. If you choose not to use Beyond Meat, save the taco seasoning packet for later.
Prepare the enchilada sauce according to the packet directions using the tomato sauce.

In a large mixing bowl, add the rice, beans, quinoa, chopped green onions (don't add all your onion; save a few pinches to put on top), 1 cup of the enchilada sauce, diced Roma tomato, jalapeño, Beyond Meat mixture and the cilantro. If you did not to use Beyond Meat, sprinkle in half the taco seasoning mix at this step. Mix together. Add salt and pepper to taste. Mix again. Coat a casserole dish with olive oil. Press the mixture into the casserole dish and smooth it out. Top with a small amount of the remaining enchilada sauce. Sprinkle the top with the sliced olives and remaining green onions.

Bake for about 25 minutes.

Serve with diced avocado on the side.

Hoppin' John

From the kitchen of Deanna Timmen

Ingredients:

1 cup Onion, chopped
1 Sweet Red Pepper, chopped
1 cup cooked Ham Steak or left over Holiday Ham, chopped
2 Tbsp Vegetable Oil
2 15.5-oz cans of Bush's Blackeye Peas with Bacon
½ to 1 tsp Hot Pepper Sauce
3 cups of cooked White Rice
Toppings: Salsa and Sour cream, for serving

Instructions:

In a large skillet, cook the onion, red pepper, and ham in oil for about 4 minutes, or until vegetables are crisp-tender.
Drain the blackeye peas, reserving about ½ cup of the liquid.
Add the blackeye peas, reserved liquid, and hot pepper sauce to the ham mixture; stir to combine and heat through.
Spoon over cooked rice.
Top with salsa and sour cream, if desired.

Marry Me Chicken

From the kitchen of Juanita Diaz

Ingredients:

2 Tbsp Extra-Virgin Olive Oil
4 boneless, skinless Chicken Breasts (2 pounds)
3-4 cloves Garlic, minced
1 cup Heavy Whipping Cream
½ cup Chicken Stock or Broth
1 tsp Chicken Better Than Bouillon or 1 cube Chicken Bouillon
½ cup Grated Parmesan Cheese (or as much as you like)
1 7-oz jar Sun Dried Tomatoes, drained and roughly chopped
1 tsp Italian Seasoning
Salt & Pepper, to taste
½ tsp Red Peppers, to taste
¼ cup Basil Leaves, thinly sliced

Instructions:

Pat chicken dry and season all over with salt. Heat the oil in a large skillet over medium heat; once pan is hot, add chicken and cook on each side 5-7 minutes depending on thickness-until golden brown. Place aside on plate when cooked.
Add garlic to the same skillet and cook until fragrant, about 30-40 seconds. Stir in heavy cream, chicken stock, bouillon, ¼ cup (or as much as you like) parmesan cheese, sundried tomatoes, Italian seasoning, pepper, red pepper flakes and salt to taste. Place chicken in the cream sauce, and simmer, turn heat down to low. Cover and cook for about 7-10 minutes longer. Make sure chicken is completely cooked and tender. Add more cream or cheese if needed. Top chicken with basil leaves, parmesan cheese and pasta or mashed potatoes. Serves 4 people.

Crispy Chicken Katsu (Japanese Cutlet)

From the kitchen of Michi Arakawa

Ingredients:

1 ½ lbs Chicken Breasts or Thighs, skinless and boneless (cut to ½ inch thick slices)
2 Eggs, beaten
¾ cup Flour
½ tsp Garlic Powder
2 ½ cups Panko (Japanese dried breadcrumbs)
1 quart Avocado Oil, for deep frying in saucepan (equivalent of 1 inch of oil)

Tonkatsu Sauce:
⅓ cup Catsup
2 ½ Tbsp Worcestershire sauce
1 Tbsp Shoyu
1 Tbsp Brown Sugar or ½ tsp white sugar
⅛ tsp Garlic and Onion Powder (optional)

Instructions:

Prepare 3 shallow bowls for flour, eggs and panko.
Dredge chicken in flour/garlic mixture. Shake off excess.
Dip floured chicken in egg mixture. Let excess drip off.
Coat completely with panko. Shake off excess and put on plate.
Heat oil medium-high until 350°F. Fry approximately 3-4 minutes per side until golden brown and 165°F inside. Cool on paper towels on plate or wire rack. Mix together Tonkatsu Sauce ingredients. Serve chilled with chicken katsu.

Lumpiang Shanghai (Ground Pork Lumpia)

Anonymous

Ingredients:

50 Pieces Lumpia wrapper
3 cups Cooking Oil
1 Egg (beaten-use to seal the lumpia)

Filling:
1 ½ lbs Ground Pork
2 medium Onions, minced
2 medium Carrots, minced
1 ½ tsp Garlic Powder
½ tsp Ground Black Pepper
½ cup Green Onion, chopped
1 ½ tsp Salt
1 Tbsp Sesame Oil
2 Eggs

Instructions:

Combine all filling ingredients in a bowl. Mix well. Cover and rest mixture for 30 minutes in the fridge.
Before wrapping, separate the lumpia wrappers and cover with cloth to keep from drying out. Scoop about 1 to 1 ½ Tbsp of filling and place onto a piece of lumpia wrapper. (One corner of the wrapper pointing towards you, in diamond formation).
Spread the filling and then fold both sides of the wrapper. Fold the bottom, brush beaten egg mixture on the top end of the wrapper.
Roll up until completely wrapped. (See back of the lumpia wrapper package for wrapping instruction). Refrigerate until ready to cook.

Frying:
Heat oil in a cooking pot. Deep fry lumpia on medium heat until it floats.
Remove from the pot and put them in a strainer. Let excess oil drip.
Serve with Sweet & Spicy sauce (store bought dipping sauce).

Pastetli (Pastry Shells)

From the kitchen of Heidi Blake

Ingredients:

1 package Pepperidge Farm Puff Pastry Shells
4 boneless Chicken Breasts, cut up
2-3 Tbsp Half & Half or Cream
2-3 tbsp Corn Starch/Water mixture
2 cloves Garlic, crushed
¼ cup Chardonay Wine
½ tsp Poultry Seasoning
½ tsp ground Black Pepper
½ Onion, chopped
1 lb Mushrooms, sliced
1 cube Knorr Chicken Bouillon
1 can Cream of Chicken or Mushroom Soup
1 cup Water

Instructions:

Bake pastry shells as directed on package, and remove 10 minutes before done to cut lids out and remove with fork or sharp knife. Return back to oven to finish baking shells and lids until golden brown.
Meanwhile, cook chicken pieces in skillet. Divide into 2 portions and set aside. In same pan, sauté onion, garlic and mushrooms until tender. Add white wine and cook for 5 minutes. Add cream of chicken or mushroom soup. Dissolve bouillon cube in 1 cup of warm water, before adding. Add seasonings and gently stir until creamy gravy forms. Add half & half or cream to enrich if desired. Serve in pastry shells.
**Note: it was a traditional Christmas Eve dinner at our house in Switzerland.

Enchiladas Suizas Flojas (Lazy Swiss Enchiladas)

From the kitchen of Jennifer Blake Rivera

Ingredients:

Sauce:
10 Tomatillos, husked and rinsed
2-3 Jalapeño/Serrano Chiles (seeded if you want it milder)
¼ cup raw White Onion, diced
3-4 Garlic cloves
½ cup Mexican Crema or Sour Cream
½ cup fresh Cilantro with stems, chopped
1 8-ounce package of Cream Cheese
Chicken Bouillon to taste
Water/Chicken Broth if you have it available
Salt, to taste

Enchiladas:
Cooked shredded Chicken (boiled or rotisserie works great)
12-15 corn tortillas
1 cup Shredded Cheese (Monterey Jack, Oaxaca, or Mozzarella)
Vegetable Oil (for softening tortillas)

Optional Toppings:
Sliced avocado, thinly sliced onion

Instructions:

Make the Green Sauce: Add tomatillos and chiles to a pot and cover with water.
Boil for 5–7 minutes, until tomatillos soften and mostly turn a dull green (a bit of bright green will give you a bit more tang and is totally okay).

In blender or food processor, add raw onion and raw garlic, and blend quickly until they are chopped. Remove tomatillos and chiles from pot, using a bit of the water they were boiled in, and add to onion/garlic mix. Add cilantro, water or chicken broth, chicken bouillon, crema, and cream cheese and blend everything until smooth. Taste and adjust salt, if needed.

Add a bit of oil to large deep pan, add mixture from blender and heat sauce through. Let simmer on low so sauce stays warm while assembling enchiladas.

Prepare the Filling: Shred chicken in large bowl. Add enough sauce to chicken to coat and flavor chicken. Salt to taste, if needed.

Soften the Tortillas: Heat oil in a skillet over medium heat. Lightly fry each tortilla for 5-10 seconds per side until soft (not crispy). Place on a paper towel.

Assemble the Enchiladas: Preheat oven to 375°F (190°C). Spread a thin layer of green sauce on the bottom of a baking dish. Add chicken filling to each tortilla, roll it up, and place in the dish (seam-side down).

Add Sauce & Cheese: Pour remaining green sauce over the rolled tortillas. Lightly sprinkle more shredded cheese evenly on top.

Bake 15-20 minutes, until the cheese is melted and bubbling. I like to turn on the broiler for a few minutes so the top gets golden (careful to set a timer so they don't burn!)

Top with crema, avocado slices, cilantro, or sliced raw onions. Serve hot.

Uncle Bock's San Antonio Style Enchiladas

From the kitchen of Deanna Timmen

Ingredients:

2 lbs Ground Beef or Chicken (or shredded Rotisserie Chicken)
½ Onion, diced
1 tsp Seasoning Salt
1 Bay Leaf
3 Garlic Cloves, minced

Spices:
1 tsp Cumin
1 tsp Garlic Powder
½ tsp Onion Powder
2 Tbsp Chili Powder
1 Enchilada Seasoning Packet (optional)

Sauce base:
1 can tomato paste + 2–4 cans water (to make it soupy) or 2 cans tomato sauce

Cheese:
3 cups Sharp Cheddar, shredded
3 cups Colby Jack, shredded

Instructions:

Preheat oven to 300°F. Spray a 9x13 inch baking dish. Soften tortillas: quick-fry in about ¾ inch of oil (about 1 second per side) or warm on a greased griddle.
Make meat sauce: cook meat, onion, garlic and seasonings; add tomato paste/water (or tomato sauce) and simmer low 30+ minutes. Remove bay leaf; discard.

Assemble: fill each tortilla with a little cheese and meat sauce; roll tight; place seam-side down in a single layer. Top with remaining sauce, then cheese.
Cover with foil. Bake 15 minutes. Uncover; bake another 10–15 minutes more until bubbly and melted. Rest a few minutes, then serve.

**Optional time-savers:
Use Costco rotisserie chicken; pulse in a food processor for "ground" texture.
Shortcut sauce: El Paso Enchilada sauce + tomato sauce.
Shred cheese fast with a food processor.

Adobo Chicken

From the kitchen of JD DeLeon

Ingredients:

6-8 Chicken pieces (Bone-in, skin-on thighs, legs, or whole cut-up chicken)
½ cup Soy Sauce
¼ cup Vinegar: White vinegar, rice vinegar, or cane vinegar
6 cloves Garlic, minced
3 Bay Leaves
1 tsp whole Black Peppercorns
1 cup Water

Common Additions & Variations:
1-2 Tbsp Brown sugar, Honey, or even Pineapple soda
½ Onions, sliced
½ cup Coconut Milk: Adds richness and creamier version

Instructions:

Marinate chicken with soy sauce, vinegar, garlic, bay leaves, and peppercorns. Pour chicken and marinade into skillet or wok. Sear chicken until browned on each side for color and flavor.
Braise chicken in the marinade and other liquids (water/coconut milk), and simmer, covered until chicken is tender. (23 -28 minutes on medium heat)
The sauce is often reduced to a rich glaze or add a tablespoon of cornstarch for sauce thickness. Remove and discard bay leaves and whole peppercorns before serving.
Serves 4 people.

Grandma Flora's Ravioli

From the kitchen of Greg Barrett

Ingredients:

Pasta Dough:
5 cups Flour (Italian "Tipo 00" for pasta is ideal)
3 tsp Salt
4 Eggs, beaten
1 to 1 ½ cups tepid water (add slowly)
2 Tbsp Olive Oil

Filling:
1 cup Cottage Cheese
2 boxes frozen chopped Spinach, thawed and squeeze excess water out
1 lb Ground Beef
½ lb Ground Veal or Lamb
½ lb Italian Pork Sausage
3 eggs, beaten
1 cup grated Parmigiano-Reggiano (or just Parmesan)
Salt & Pepper to taste

Instructions:

Make pasta dough by creating a volcano-shape with the flour on a large cutting board or clean counter. Sprinkle with salt. Add eggs & oil into center of volcano. Knead dough as you gradually add water. Add more water if it is too dry and crumbles. If it becomes too sticky, add flour. Cover with plastic wrap and let rest.
Meanwhile, to create filling, brown meats in skillet; drain; cool then run through food processor to become fine. In large bowl, mix the cheeses, spinach, meat and seasonings. Add eggs. Mix until well blended. Set aside.

Return to the dough. Roll out chunks of dough as thin as possible into a sheet, in order to create several ravioli. (You will need to ravioli cutter or ravioli maker press-mold to make your life easier). Place small amounts of filling into center of each ravioli. Lay another sheet of dough on top. Roll firmly over filled dough with the ravioli cutter (or rolling pin over the press-mold). Gently work the ravioli's apart from each other and press edges to make sure they are securely closed.
Place on parchment paper lined pan to freeze briefly until able to safely stack layers on top of each other or to transfer to large Ziplock bags. Store in freezer until time to cook for dinner.
When you are ready to cook ravioli, gently boil in water for 3-5 minutes. They should float when done. Transfer to serving bowl and apply desired sauce. Marinara, alfredo, pesto or meat sauce go great!

MeLinda's Famous Smoked Turkey & Greens

From the kitchen of MeLinda Harvey

Ingredients:

4 bundles of Collard Greens
4 bundles of Turnip Greens
4 bundles of Mustard Greens
1 large Onion, quartered
5-6 Garlic cloves, crushed (or minced Garlic about 2-4 Tbsp)
3-4 Tbsp Bacon fat (adds an extra layer of flavor)
3 large Smoked (pre-cooked) Turkey Legs or Wings
6-8 cups Water to create Turkey Stock (or substitute with water and chicken bouillon, if preferred)
Creole Kick seasoning, to taste
1 Jalapeño (optional for more spice)

Instructions:

Make the broth with Turkey: Start by building your broth - This is where a lot of your flavor is going to come from, so don't rush it. Place the smoked turkey legs or wings into a large pot. (I use the Instant-Pot.) Pour in 6-8 cups of water to cover the meat completely. Bring it to a boil - Once you see a steady boil, turn down the heat to low. Let it simmer for about 1 hour, until the turkey legs are tender and the meat is practically falling off the bone.

Remove the turkey legs or wings from pot. Set them aside to cool slightly. Once cool enough to handle, shred the turkey meat off the bone. Reserve the flavorful cooking liquid (broth) for your greens.

Prep and wash the greens: While the turkey is simmering, wash the collard, turnip and mustard greens thoroughly. Trim away any tough stems. (Although collard stems are edible, they can be fibrous, so removing them helps the greens cook down better.) Roughly chop your greens into bite-sized pieces. Set them aside to drain.

Heat the Bacon fat in a large, heavy pot or Dutch oven, over medium heat. (Bacon fat is the secret ingredient that gives the greens a deep, smoky flavor.) Once hot, sauté the onions and garlic for about 3-5 minutes, or until the onions are translucent and the garlic smells deliciously fragrant.

Pour the reserved cooking broth into the pot. Add the shredded turkey. Gradually add greens in batches, stirring as they start to wilt down. Don't rush; let each handful cook down a bit before adding more.

Season it up - Sprinkle in your Creole Kick seasoning to taste, along with chopped jalapeño if you like a bit of heat. Simmer low and slow, once everything's in the pot, for 1.5 to 2 hours. This is where they turn tender and soak up all that smoky, savory goodness.

Stir occasionally and add more liquid if needed to keep the greens from sticking.

Taste and adjust - Before serving, give the greens a taste and adjust the seasoning if needed. A little extra Creole Kick or a pinch of salt can make all the difference.

For the full Southern experience, don't forget the cornbread on the side and I add a splash of apple cider vinegar on top for brightness.

**Try smoked ham hocks if you don't have smoked turkey - Ham hocks work just as well and bring a similar smoky flavor.

Use chicken bouillon for an extra savory broth - Bouillon cubes or paste can add an extra layer of flavor to the broth.

Leftovers are even better - Greens taste even better the next day, so make enough to enjoy later.

Lennaea's Christmas Morning Frittata

From the Kitchen of Lennaea Sood

Ingredients:

28-oz Bag of Frozen Potatoes O'Brien
½ cup Butter (1 stick)
13-oz Hillshire Farm Smoked Turkey Polska Kielbasa, cubed
10 Eggs
2 cups Shredded Cheddar Jack Cheese
Salt, Pepper & Johnny's Seasoning to taste

Optional Item: Diced Green Onions

Instructions:

Pre-heat oven to 350°F. May to need to increase heat as needed depending on oven.
In a large casserole dish, lay out potatoes and spread them in dish. Season potatoes to liking using salt, pepper & Johnny's Seasoning Salt. Cut up butter and place randomly over potatoes. Place in oven until butter is melted, then remove.
Whisk eggs and 1 cup of shredded cheese, and salt and pepper to taste in separate bowl-set aside for now. Sprinkle 1 cup of Shredded Cheese over Potatoes.
Cut up small cubes of Turkey Kielbasa and sprinkle them over cheese.
Final Step is to pour mixed eggs & cheese over the whole thing. Do not cover. Place in oven and bake for up to 45 minutes or until center is no longer runny.

Crockpot Creamy Chicken Pasta

From the kitchen of Lennaea Sood

Ingredients:

6 Boneless Chicken Breasts (or shredded pre-cooked rotisserie chicken to save time)
½ cup of Butter
1-oz Package of Italian Seasoning or Italian Salad Dressing Mix
1 can Golden Mushroom Soup
4-oz Chive & Onion Cream Cheese
Noodles of Choice
Pepper & Johnny's Seasoning Salt, to taste

Instructions:

Put chicken in crockpot and seasoning to chicken as needed. (I usually add Johnny's Seasoning Salt and Pepper.)
Melt butter in a saucepan and add all other ingredients. Stir ingredients and once mixed together, pour over chicken in crockpot and let cook on low for 5-6 hours. Shred chicken. This recipe can also be sped up by cooking all ingredients on stove top in a Dutch Oven.
Boil pasta of choice. Strain out water. Pour crockpot chicken over pasta.
We use fettuccine noodles or Spaghetti Noodles. But it also goes great over rice.

Super Easy Creamy Spaghetti

From the Kitchen of Lennaea Sood

Ingredients:

32-oz Jar of Rao's Homemade Marinara
15-oz Jar of Rao's Homemade Alfredo Sauce
1 lb of Ground Turkey
16-oz box of Spaghetti Noodles
1 cup Fresh Parmesan
Salt & Pepper, to taste

Instructions:

In a large saucepan or Dutch Oven, brown ground turkey in pan and season with salt & pepper. Once cooked, add jar of Marinara and jar of Alfredo Sauce. Turn heat to low and let sauces slowly heat through.
Boil Spaghetti noodles according to box instructions, drain and then add to sauce.
Sprinkle with fresh Parmesan and serve.
Enjoy with rolls, sourdough bread or garlic bread.

Authentic Liberian Cassava Leaf

From the kitchen of Edwina Kamara & MeLinda Harvey

Ingredients:

3 1-lb packs of frozen Cassava Leaves (found in most International grocery stores or farmers markets)
1-2 lbs of a variety of meats - Chicken, Beef and/or Shrimp
2-3 pieces of Dried Fish
1 Onion, chopped
1 Scotch Bonnet Pepper (optional - if spice is desired)
½ - 1 cup Palm Oil
Chicken and Maggi Shrimp Bouillon cubes
Seasoning Salt and other seasonings of your choice, to taste

Instructions:

Cube and pre-season meats with seasoning salt. For best results, let seasoned meats sit overnight in refrigerator.
In a large pot, add meat (except shrimp), dried fish, onions, bouillon cubes and enough water to cover the meat. Bring to a boil.
When meat is almost fully cooked, add the cassava leaves into the pot. If cooking with shrimp, you may add it at any time while cassava leaves are cooking.
Add additional seasonings and bouillon cubes, to taste.
Boil all ingredients together for about 25 minutes or until water is almost diminished. (You will need to check the water frequently so it doesn't dry up).
When the water is almost diminished, add the palm oil and cook for another 5 minutes.

Serve over rice.

Soups & Stews

"Is it not to share your food with the hungry and to provide the poor wanderer with shelter…?" Isaiah 58:7

White Chicken Chili

From the kitchen of Kristen Barrett

Ingredients:

3 boneless Chicken breasts
1 can each of Kidney Beans & Black Beans, rinsed and drained
1 can Pinto/Chili Beans, undrained
1 can Yellow Corn, drained
1 can RO-TEL diced tomatoes & green chilies (add another can if you want more of a tomato base)
1 8-oz package Cream Cheese
1 packet White Chicken Chili Seasoning mix (*see homemade substitution below)
1 packet Ranch Dressing mix

*Homemade Seasoning Substitute:
1 tsp Cumin
1 tsp Chili Powder
½ tsp Garlic Powder
½ tsp Onion Powder
½ tsp Smoked Paprika
½ tsp Dried Oregano
Salt & Pepper, to taste

Instructions:

Place chicken in bottom of crockpot, pour all other ingredients on top of chicken. Cook low 6-8 hours. Remove chicken to shred on cutting board with two forks. Return shredded chicken back into crockpot and stir. Cook an additional 20-30 minutes to allow chicken to absorb all of the flavor. Serve with Sour Cream, Shredded Mexican blend cheese, Fritos or Tortilla Strips.

Clam Chowder

From the kitchen of Heidi Blake

Ingredients:

1 quart Milk (or Half & Half is even better)
4 cans of minced Clams, save the juice as well
5 large Russett Potatoes or equivalent in Red Potatoes, cubed
1 large Onion, diced
4 stalks of Celery, diced
½ pound Bacon, sliced
1 8-oz can of whole Kernel Corn, drained
1 8-oz can Creamed Corn
½ cube of Butter
2 Tbsp Fresh Parsley
1 clove Garlic, minced
Salt & Pepper, to taste

Instructions:

Boil potatoes until slightly tender. Drain and set aside. Sauté bacon until brown. Remove onto paper towel. Using remaining bacon grease, sauté celery and onion until tender. In large soup pot, melt butter, add garlic and parsley. Simmer 1 min on low (don't let butter burn). Then add clams with it's juice, then stir. Add all other ingredients. Continue to heat on low until thick. Season to taste. If needed to thicken more, use basic cornstarch & water method.

Mexican Pozole Rojo

From the kitchen of Kristen Barrett

Ingredients:

2 lbs Pork Carnita meat, cubed into 2-inch chunks
1 White Onion, diced
8 cloves Garlic, minced (or 4 tsp Crushed Garlic)
8 cups Beef Broth
1 small can Tomato Paste
2 30-oz cans of Gold Hominy
½ tsp White Vinegar
2 ounces Ancho Chile powder or Las Palmas Red Chile Sauce
2 ounces dried Guajillo Chile powder
1-2 Tbsp Arbol Chile powder (optional for increased spice level)
Salt, to taste (up to 1 Tbsp)
2 Tbsp Cumin
2 Tbsp Mexican Oregano

Toppings at serving: Cilantro, diced avocado, lime wedges, radishes, diced onion (white or green), shredded cabbage, cotija cheese, Mexican crema or sour cream.

Instructions:

Make chile sauce: mix chile powders with tomato paste and 1 cup of the beef broth. Place cubed pork, Chile sauce and other ingredients (excluding the toppings items) in a large crockpot on low for 6-8 hours or high 4-5 hours, until pork is softened enough to shred.
Once pork is tender, shred with two forks on a cutting board and return to crockpot to simmer another 20 minutes.
Serve with toppings on the side. Serves 10-12 people.

Spicy Chicken Taco Soup

From the kitchen of Donna Kennedy

Ingredients:

4-6 Chicken Breasts, thinly sliced
1 each Red, Yellow and Orange Bell Peppers
2 Sweet Onions
2 cans Ro-Tel diced tomatoes & green chilies
1 large can Mild Green Chiles
1 can Black Beans
1 small can Tomato Paste
4 cups Chicken Stock, or enough to cover ingredients
2 Tbsp Cumin
1½ Tbsp Cayenne Pepper
¾ Tbsp Red Pepper Flakes

Optional Toppings: Avocado, Cilantro, Limes, tortilla strips or Fritos corn chips

Instructions:

Line the bottom of a 6-quart crockpot with thinly cut chicken breasts.
Heavily season the chicken with cumin, cayenne pepper and red pepper flakes, to taste.
On top of the chicken add roughly diced red, yellow and orange peppers. Add diced onions. Add Ro-Tel and mild green chiles. Add a can of well-rinsed black beans. Cook on low 6-8 hours. Remove chicken to shred with two forks and return to crockpot. Mix well and serve.

Grandma Margaret's Inspired Potato Soup

From the kitchen of Candice Ashby

Ingredients:

¼ cup White Onion, diced
3 cloves Garlic, minced
5 strips Bacon
7 Golden Potatoes, peeled (optional), washed, and diced
½ Tbsp Old Bay seasoning
1 tsp ground Sea Salt
1 tsp Parsley
1 tsp Garlic Powder
½ tsp ground Black Pepper
1 12-oz can Evaporated Milk
½ cup Heavy Whipping Cream
5 cups Chicken Broth (as needed for simmering)

Optional Toppings: Shredded Cheddar Cheese and Bacon bits

Instructions:

In a large pot or Dutch oven, cook the bacon over medium heat until almost crispy.
Remove, crumble and set aside. Leave about 1–2 Tbsp of bacon fat in the pot. Add diced onion to the pot and sauté until soft (about 3–4 minutes).
Stir in garlic and cook for another 30 seconds. Add diced potatoes, Old Bay, salt, parsley, garlic powder, and black pepper. Stir well to coat everything. Add 5 cups of chicken broth to just cover the potatoes. Bring to a boil, then reduce heat and simmer for 15–20 minutes, or until potatoes are fork-tender.

Make it creamy by pouring in the evaporated milk and heavy cream. Stir and let it gently heat through (do not boil). Use a potato masher to mash some of the potatoes directly in the pot for a thicker, creamier texture. Leave some chunks for texture. Stir in most of the crumbled bacon, saving some for topping. Ladle into bowls and top with shredded cheddar cheese and remaining bacon bits.

**Pair with a salad and/or some yummy French bread and enjoy!

Zuppa Toscana (Olive Garden Copycat)

From the kitchen of Juanita Diaz

Ingredients:

1 lb ground Italian Sausage (mild or spicy)
3-4 cloves Garlic, minced
1 medium White Onion, diced
4-5 Yukon Gold Potatoes, diced (about 1.5 pounds)
5-6 cups Chicken Stock
2-3 cups fresh Kale, chopped
1 cup Heavy Whipping Cream
½ cup Parmesan Cheese
Salt, Pepper, Italian Seasoning, Onion Powder, Garlic Powder, to taste
7 pieces Bacon, cooked crumbled/chopped

Instructions:

Cook sausage in large stock pot over medium heat until brown and cooked through; break into small pieces. Take sausage out of pot with slotted spoon; reserve 1 Tbsp grease in pot. Add onions and sauté until translucent. Add garlic and cook until fragrant. Add potatoes, chicken stock, and cooked sausage, cook until it reaches a simmer. Reduce heat to medium-low and simmer for 10 minutes or until potatoes are fork tender. Stir in kale, cream, parmesan cheese, and seasoning to taste. Serve and garnish with bacon bits.
Serves 8 people.

Fowl Stew –

a Hearty Crowd Pleaser of All Things Poultry

From the kitchen of Nina ThyNguyen

Ingredients:

2 Tbsp Butter
2 Tbsp Olive Oil
1 medium Onion, diced
2 medium Carrots, peeled and diced
3 stalks Celery, diced
4 Garlic cloves, minced
½ tsp Sweet Paprika
Salt and Black Pepper, to taste
3 Tbsp All-Purpose Flour
4 cups Chicken Broth
1 Tbsp Apple Cider Vinegar
1 lb Turkey, ground
1 lb Chicken, ground
1½ lbs boneless, skinless Chicken Thighs, cubed
1 lb Chicken Apple Sausage, cut into ½ inch pieces
½ tsp fresh Sage, minced
½ tsp fresh Thyme, minced
½ tsp fresh Oregano, minced
1 lb Turkey Bacon, cooked and crumbled, then cooled and set aside for serving
Fresh Parsley, minced, for serving

Instructions:

Heat a large pot or Dutch oven over medium. Add butter, olive oil, and onion. Cook, stirring frequently, until onion is translucent, 5 to 7 minutes.

Add flour and stir for 1 minute. Add chicken broth and vinegar and stir until flour is incorporated. Next, add garlic, paprika, carrots, and celery. Cook, stirring occasionally for 5 minutes. Add chicken thighs, ground chicken and turkey, chicken sausages, sage, thyme, oregano, and 1 teaspoon each of salt and black pepper. Bring the stew to a gentle boil on medium-high and then reduce heat to maintain a simmer. Simmer, with a lid partially covering the pot, until the chicken is cooked through, for about 20 minutes.

Season to taste with more salt and pepper. Serve in bowls, garnished with parsley and crumbled turkey bacon.

**Note: The stew can be frozen for up to 3 months, then defrosted for easy reheating. Dried herbs can be substituted.

Desserts

"How sweet are Your words to my taste, sweeter than honey to my mouth!" Psalm 119:103

The Ultimate Creamy Banana Pudding

From the kitchen of Patience Edwards

Ingredients:

2 cups cold Whole Milk
2 packs (5.1-oz each) Instant Vanilla Pudding mix
1 14-oz can Sweetened Condensed Milk
1 tsp Vanilla Extract
1 tub (12-oz) Frozen whipped topping (like Cool Whip), thawed

The Layers:
1 box Vanilla Wafers (Nilla Wafers are the classic choice)
1 bag Chessmen Butter Cookies (for that decorative top layer)
5-6 Ripe bananas, sliced into rounds

Optional : Caramel sauce for drizzling

Instructions:

Mix the Pudding: In a large bowl , whisk together the cold milk and the two packs of instant vanilla pudding mix for about 2 minutes until it starts to thicken.
Fold in the sweetened condensed milk and vanilla extract until the mixture is smooth and pale yellow.
Make it Fluffy by gently folding in about half of the thawed whipped topping. This gives the pudding that airy, mousse-like consistency.
The First Layer: In a large trifle bowl or a 9x13 baking dish, place a single layer of vanilla wafers at the bottom. Top with a layer of sliced bananas.
Build the Middle: Pour half of the pudding mixture over the bananas, spreading it to the edges. Repeat with another layer of wafers, bananas, and the remaining pudding.

The Topping: Spread the remaining whipped topping over the top. Arrange the Chessmen butter cookies in a neat grid across the surface.

The Secret Step: For the best texture, cover and refrigerate for at least 4 hours (overnight is even better). This allows the cookies to soften into a cake-like texture.

Just before serving, add a few fresh banana slices and a drizzle of caramel sauce if you want that extra "gourmet" look.

German Apple Cake

From the kitchen of Heidi Blake

Ingredients:

4 cups raw Apples, diced
2 cups Sugar
2 tsp Vanilla
2 tsp Baking Soda
1 tsp Salt
2 Eggs
½ cup Vegetable Oil
½ cup Flour
2 tsp Cinnamon
½ cup chopped Nuts

Whipped Topping:
1 3-oz package Cream Cheese
$^{2}/_{3}$ cups Margaine or Butter, softened
1 tsp Vanilla Extract
1 ½ cups Powdered Sugar

Instructions:

Preheat oven to 350°F. Mix sugar, eggs, oil and vanilla. Pour over apples and nuts. In separate bowl, mix flour, baking soda, cinnamon and salt. Add to apple mixture. Mix well. Pour into 9x13 inch cake pan. Bake for 60 minutes.
When cool, apply whipped topping (can be substituted with Cool Whip if desired).
**Note: Since the cake is rich, I'd use a tart apple like Granny Smith or Pink Lady, but Honey Crisp or Cosmic Crisp would be great too.

Birchermüesli

From the kitchen of Heidi Blake

Ingredients:

1 cup Quick-Cook Oats
1 Berry Yoplait Yogurt
1 cup Milk
2-3 Granny Smith or Braeburn Apples
1 cup fresh or frozen Strawberries, sliced
2 Bananas, sliced
2 Oranges, sliced to bite-size
1 8-oz can Diced Pineapple
1 8-oz can Fruit Cocktail (optional)
½ cup finely ground Nuts
½ cup Sugar
2 cups Heavy Whipping Cream
Juice of 1 Lemon
1 cup Granola

Instructions:

In large bowl, mix oats, milk, yogurt, sugar, lemon juice and ground nuts. Peel and shred apples. Add to mixture. Add remaining fruit, granola and 1 cup whipping cream. Mix well. Place in serving dish. Whip remaining cup of whipping cream until fluffy. Decorate top of mixture with whipped cream and berries.

**Note: It can also be served with breakfast in summer.

Gingersnap Cookies

From the kitchen of Kristen Barrett

Ingredients:

2 cups Flour
2 tsp Baking Soda
1 tsp Cinnamon
½ tsp Nutmeg
½ tsp Salt
¾ cup Shortening
1 Egg, slightly beaten
¼ cup Dark Molasses
1 cup Granulated Sugar
1 Tbsp fresh Ginger, minced
½ cup cinnamon-sugar blend, to coat dough balls

Instructions:

Preheat oven to 350°F. Mix the first five dry ingredients in a bowl. In separate bowl, beat shortening until creamy. Add sugar, egg, molasses and ginger. Slowly add flour mixture until well blended.
Pinch off small amounts of dough and roll into 1-inch balls. Roll dough balls in a shallow dish of cinnamon-sugar mixture until evenly coated and place on ungreased cookie sheets.
Bake for 10 minutes. Remove cookies from pan and cool on wire rack.
Makes about 3 dozen cookies.

Mom's Huckleberry Cream Pie

From the kitchen of Kristen Barrett

Ingredients:

1 9-inch Shortbread Pie Shell
1 8-oz package Cream Cheese
1 cup Powdered Sugar
1 tsp Vanilla Extract
½ pint Heavy Whipping Cream (or Cool Whip)
2 cups Huckleberries, fresh or frozen
1 cup Granulated Sugar
½ cup Water
3 Tbsp Cornstarch

Instructions:

Mix cream cheese, powdered sugar and vanilla. Spread cream mixture onto bottom of pie shell. Refrigerate.
Meanwhile, in sauce pan, combine huckleberries, sugar, water and cornstarch. Bring to a boil, stirring constantly. Cook until thickened, then cool.
Pour over cream cheese mixture in pie shell. Whip the heavy whipping cream (or use Cool Whip substitute) and gently spread over berry mixture. You can sprinkle a few fresh huckleberries on top for added pizazz. Refrigerate until ready to serve.
Makes 8 standard slices.

Oh So Rich Peanut Butter Pie

From the kitchen of Heidi Blake

Ingredients:

Filling:
2 cups Powdered Sugar
$^2/_3$ cup Peanut Butter (creamy or chunky- your choice)
1 8-oz package Cream Cheese, softened
2 small containers of Cool Whip, thawed

Graham Cracker Crust:
1 ½ Graham Crackers, finely crumbled
1 Tbsp Granulated Sugar
¼ cup Chopped Nuts (Optional)
¾ cup Butter, melted

Optional Toppings:
Reese's Pieces, Toffee crumbles or crushed Butterfinger candy

Instructions:

Preheat oven to 375°F. Mix graham cracker crust ingredients and pack evenly along bottom of two 8-inch pie pans. Bake for 10 minutes. (Or substitute for 2 store-bought graham cracker pie crusts.)
In large bowl, cream together first 3 filling ingredients. This mixture is very stiff… use your mixer slowly or a very strong spoon. Stir in cool whip, blend with mixer until smooth. Pour into two cooled 8-inch graham cracker pie crusts.
Top with Reese's Pieces candy (crumbled), Toffee crumbles or crushed Butterfinger bits of your choice. Chill 4-6 hours or best if overnight.

Black Forest Tiramisu

From the kitchen of Mona Borgens & Kristen Barrett

Ingredients:

Base:
15 Italian Ladyfingers (Savoiardi)
1 cup strong Espresso (cooled)
2 Tbsp Granulated Sugar
1 Tbsp Coffee Liqueur (optional)

Mascarpone Cream:
2 Egg Yolks
¼ cup Sugar (divided)
2 ¼ cups (18 ounces) Mascarpone Cheese, room temperature
½ cup Heavy Whipping Cream
2 tsp Vanilla Extract or Vanilla Bean Paste
Pinch of Salt

Cherry Mixture:
½ cup Cherry Puree (fresh or frozen, thawed cherries–blend then drain excess liquid)
Splash of Cherry Liqueur (optional)

Topping:
2 ounces Dark Chocolate (70–75%), shaved
2 ounces White Chocolate, shaved
Cocoa Powder (for dusting)
Maraschino Cherries or fresh Cherries (optional garnish)

Optional Espresso substitution for non-coffee drinkers:
1 packet Hot Chocolate Cocoa mix
Splash of Vanilla Extract
6 ounces Hot Water

Instructions:

Prepare coffee mixture in a shallow bowl, by stirring together espresso, sugar, and coffee liqueur until dissolved. Set aside.
In a heat-proof bowl, whisk egg yolks with 2 Tbsp sugar. Place over a pot of simmering water (creating double boiler). Whisk continuously for 3–5 minutes until pale, slightly thickened, and smooth. Remove from heat and let cool slightly.
In a separate bowl, beat mascarpone cheese until smooth. Add remaining sugar, vanilla and salt. Mix until fully combined. Stir egg yolk mixture into mascarpone mixture.
In another bowl, whip heavy cream to soft peaks. Gently fold in whipped cream into mascarpone mixture until light and airy.
Assemble Tiramisu layers: Quickly dip each ladyfinger into coffee mixture (1–2 seconds only). Arrange in a single layer in a 9x9 inch dish.
Layer: Ladyfingers, Cherry Puree, Mascarpone cream, then Shaved chocolate.
Repeat layers once more.
Cover and refrigerate for at least 6 hours (preferably overnight).
Before serving: Dust lightly with cocoa powder. Top with chocolate curls. Garnish with maraschino or fresh cherries, if desired. Serve chilled.
Serves 8-10 people.

Pro tips:
Do not over-soak ladyfingers—they should not be soggy.
Room temperature mascarpone prevents lumps.
Overnight chilling gives the best flavor and texture.
Add a tiny pinch of flaky salt on top for a gourmet finish.

**Alternative for non-coffee fans: Mix hot chocolate packet with 6 ounces of water and a splash of vanilla extract. Cool completely. Quickly dip ladyfingers into this rather than espresso. This makes for a great kid-friendly option.

7-Up Pound Cake

From the kitchen of Juanita Diaz

Ingredients:

Cake:
1 ½ cups Unsalted Butter, at room temperature
3 cups Granulated Sugar
½ tsp Salt
5 large Eggs, room temperature
3 cups Cake Flour, sifted
½ cup 7-Up Soda
2 tsp Lemon Extract

Glaze:
1 cup Powder Sugar
3 Tbsp 7-Up Soda
½ tsp Lemon Extract

Instructions:

Preheat oven to 315°F. Liberally grease and flour bundt pan. In mixing bowl, add butter and beat for 2 minutes on high. Slowly add sugar and salt; beat on high speed for additional 7 minutes, until pale yellow and fluffy. Next, add eggs, mixing on lowest speed, and add in flour slowly; do not over-beat. Lastly, pour in 7-Up and lemon extract and mix. Pour cake batter into bundt pan and bake 1 hour and 15-20 minutes or until toothpick inserted in the center of the cake comes out clean.
Cool in pan on wire rack for about 10 minutes, then flip onto plate and remove from bundt pan. For glaze: In small bowl, whisk together powdered sugar, 7-Up and lemon extract until pourable. Drizzle on cake and allow to harden.

Banana Cake

From the kitchen of Kylie Thornton

Ingredients:

3 Eggs
2 cups Granulated Sugar
1 cup Crisco Shortening
$^{2}/_{3}$ cups Milk
1 tsp Vanilla
1 tsp Baking Powder
1 tsp Baking Soda
3 cups Flour
2-3 Bananas

Cream Cheese Frosting:
1 stick of Butter
1 8-oz package Cream Cheese
1 tsp Vanilla Extract
2 cups Powdered Sugar

Instructions:

Preheat oven 350°F. Add the eggs, sugar, Crisco, milk, vanilla, baking powder and baking soda together in a mixer. Mix well. Then, slowly add flour and bananas. Mix thoroughly. Bake for 40-50 minutes. Test with toothpick to make sure it's completely cooked through. Allow to cool.
Meanwhile, make the frosting. Mix all ingredients together in a mixer and blend until creamy. Spread cream cheese frosting on top of banana cake.

Cream Cheese Brown Sugar Fruit Dip

From the kitchen of Kylie Thornton

Ingredients:

1 8-oz package Cream Cheese, softened
¾ cups Brown Sugar
Optional: 1 tsp of Vanilla Extract

Instructions:

In a medium mixing bowl, combine the softened cream cheese, brown sugar, and vanilla extract, if using. Using a hand mixer, blend until the mixture is smooth, light, and creamy. Transfer to a decorative serving bowl and pair with your favorite assortment of fresh fruit.

Cut-Out Sugar Cookies

From the kitchen of Kylie Thornton

Ingredients:

1 cup Butter
1 cup Granulated Sugar
2 Eggs
1 tsp Vanilla Extract
1 tsp Baking Soda
1 tsp Baking Powder
2 Tbsp Milk
3 ½ cups Flour

Instructions:

Preheat oven 350°F. In large bowl, mix sugar and butter together first, then add eggs, milk, vanilla, baking powder and soda. While mixing, slowly add flour. After a bit of mixing, knead dough with hands.
Put dough on countertop and evenly roll out dough with a rolling pin until ¼ inch thick.
Take cookie cutters and stamp the dough, cutting out desired cookie shapes. Place cut-out cookies onto non-stick pan (or a pan lined with parchment paper).
Bake in oven for 7-8 minutes. Transfer to wire rack to cool.
Apply decorative frosting or glaze of your choice.

CLOSING PAGE

With an Abundantly Grateful Heart:

Psalm 128:2 says, *"You will eat the fruit of your labor; blessings and prosperity will be yours."*

To every person who contributed a recipe, shared a family favorite, or offered encouragement along the way – thank you. This cookbook is the fruit of your labor. It is your generosity, and your willingness to share something personal and meaningful.

Because of you, this collection of recipes is more than a fundraiser. It is a testimony to faith expressed through service, hospitality, and love.

May the Lord continue to bless the work of your hands. May the meals prepared from these pages nourish both body and soul of others. And may every home that opens this cookbook experience warmth, joy, and fellowship around the table.

With gratitude,

Pastor Kristen Barrett
Seattle Christian Church